The Program of Christianity

The Program of Christianity
By Henry Drummond

Start Publishing PD LLC
Copyright © 2024 by Start Publishing PD LLC

All rights reserved, including the right to reproduce this book or portions thereof in any form whatsoever.

Start Publishing PD is a registered trademark of Start Publishing PD LLC
Manufactured in the United States of America

Cover art: Shutterstock/Taisiya Kozorez

Cover design: Jennifer Do

10 9 8 7 6 5 4 3 2 1

ISBN 979-8-8809-1951-2

To Preach Good Tidings unto the Meek:

To Bind up the Broken-hearted:

To proclaim Liberty to the Captives and the Opening of the Prison to Them that are Bound:

To Proclaim the Acceptable Year of the Lord, and the Day of Vengeance of our God:

To Comfort all that Mourn:

To Appoint unto them that Mourn in Zion:

To Give unto them—

Beauty for Ashes,

The Oil of Joy for Mourning,

The Garment of Praise for the Spirit of Heaviness.

Table of Contents

The Program of Christianity 11

The Founding of the Society 18

The Program of the Society 23

The Machinery of the Society 41

The Program of Christianity

"What does God do all day?" once asked a little boy. One could wish that more grown-up people would ask so very real a question. Unfortunately, most of us are not even boys in religious intelligence, but only very unthinking children. It no more occurs to us that God is engaged in any particular work in the world than it occurs to a little child that its father does anything except be its father. Its father may be a Cabinet Minister absorbed in the nation's work, or an inventor deep in schemes for the world's good; but to this master-egoist he is father, and nothing more. Childhood, whether in the physical or moral world, is the great self-centered period of life; and a personal God who satisfies personal ends is all that for a long time many a Christian understands.

But as clearly as there comes to the growing child a knowledge of its father's part in the world, and a sense of what real life means, there must come to every Christian whose growth is true some richer sense of the meaning of Christianity and a larger view of Christ's purpose for mankind. To miss this is to miss the whole splendor and glory of Christ's religion. Next to losing the sense of a personal Christ, the worst evil that can befall a Christian is to have no sense of anything else. To grow up in complacent belief that God has no business in this great groaning world of human beings except to attend to a few saved souls is the negation of all religion. The first great epoch in a Christian's life, after the awe and wonder of its dawn, is when there breaks into his mind some sense that Christ has a purpose for mankind, a purpose beyond him and his needs, beyond the churches and their creeds, beyond Heaven and its saints—a purpose which embraces every man and woman born, every kindred and nation formed, which regards not their spiritual good alone but their welfare in every part, their progress, their health, their work, their wages, their happiness in this present world.

What, then, does Christ do all day? By what further conception shall we augment the selfish view of why Christ lived and died?

I shall mislead no one, I hope, if I say —for I wish to put the social side of Christianity in its strongest light—that Christ did not come into the world to give men religion. He never mentioned the word religion. Religion was in the world before Christ came, and it lives to-day in a million souls who have never heard His name. What God does all day is not to sit waiting in churches for people to come and worship Him. It is true that God is in churches and in all kinds of churches, and is found by many in churches more immediately than anywhere else. It is also true that while Christ did not give men religion He gave a new direction to the religious aspiration bursting forth then and now and always from the whole world's heart. But it was His purpose to enlist these aspirations on behalf of some definite practical good. The religious people of those days did nothing with their religion except attend to its observances. Even the priest, after he had been to the temple, thought his work was done; when he met the wounded man he passed by on the other side. Christ reversed all this—tried to reverse it, for He is only now beginning to succeed. The tendency of the religions of all time has been to care more for religion than for humanity; Christ cared more for humanity than for religion—rather His care for humanity was the chief expression of His religion. He was not indifferent to observances, but the practices of the people bulked in His thoughts before the practices of the Church. It has been pointed out as a blemish on the immortal allegory of Bunyan that the Pilgrim never did anything, anything but save his soul. The remark is scarcely fair, for the allegory is designedly the story of a soul in a single relation; and besides, he did do a little. But the warning may well be weighed. The Pilgrim's one thought, his work by day, his dream by night, was escape. He took little part in the world through which he passed. He was a Pilgrim traveling through it; his business was to get through safe. Whatever this is, it is not Christianity. Christ's conception of Christianity was heavens removed from that of a man setting out from the City of Destruction to save his soul. It was rather that of a man dwelling amidst the Destructions of the City and planning escapes for the souls of others—escapes not to the other world, but to purity and peace and righteousness in this. In reality Christ never said "Save your soul." It is a mistranslation which says that. What He said was, "Save your life." And this not because the first is nothing, but only because it is so very great a thing that only the second can accomplish it. But the new word altruism—the translation of "love thy neighbor as thyself"—is slowly finding its way into current Christian speech. The People's Progress, not less than the Pilgrim's Progress, is daily becoming a graver concern to the Church. A popular theology with unselfishness as part at least of its root, a theology which appeals no longer to fear, but to the generous heart in man, has already dawned, and more clearly than ever men are beginning to see what Christ really came into this world to do.

What Christ came here for was to make a better world. The world in which we live is an unfinished world. It is not wise, it is not happy, it is not pure, it is not good—it is not even sanitary. Humanity is little more than raw material. Almost everything has yet to be done to it. Before the days of Geology people thought the earth was finished. It is by no means finished. The work of Creation is going on. Before the spectroscope, men thought the universe was finished. We know now it is just beginning. And this teeming universe of men in which we live has almost all its finer color and beauty yet to take. Christ came to complete it. The fires of its passions were not yet cool; their heat had to be transformed into finer energies. The ideals for its future were all to shape, the forces to realize them were not yet born. The poison of its sins had met no antidote, the gloom of its doubt no light, the weight of its sorrow no rest. These the Savior of the world, the Light of men, would do and be. This, roughly, was His scheme.

Now this was a prodigious task—to recreate the world. How was it to be done? God's way of making worlds is to make them make themselves. When He made the earth He made a rough ball of matter and supplied it with a multitude of tools to mold it into form—the rain-drop to carve it, the glacier to smooth it, the river to nourish it, the flower to adorn it. God works always with agents, and this is our way when we want any great thing done, and this was Christ's way when He undertook the finishing of Humanity. He had a vast intractable mass of matter to deal with, and He required a multitude of tools. Christ's tools were men. Hence His first business in the world was to make a collection of men. In other words He founded a Society.

The Founding of the Society

It is a somewhat startling thought—it will not be misunderstood—that Christ probably did not save many people while He was here. Many an evangelist, in that direction, has done much more. He never intended to finish the world single-handed, but announced from the first that others would not only take part, but do "greater things" than He. For amazing as was the attention He was able to give to individuals, this was not the whole aim He had in view. His immediate work was to enlist men in His enterprise, to rally them into a great company or Society for the carrying out of His plans.

The name by which this Society was known was The Kingdom of God. Christ did not coin this name; it was an old expression, and good men had always hoped and prayed that some such Society would be born in their midst. But it was never either defined or set agoing in earnest until Christ made its realization the passion of His life.

How keenly He felt regarding His task, how enthusiastically He set about it, every page of His life bears witness. All reformers have one or two great words which they use incessantly, and by mere reiteration embed indelibly in the thought and history of their time. Christ's great word was the Kingdom of God. Of all the words of His that have come down to us this is by far the commonest. One hundred times it occurs in the Gospels. When He preached He had almost always this for a text. His sermons were explanations of the aims of His Society, of the different things it was like, of whom its membership consisted, what they were to do or to be, or not do or not be. And even when He does not actually use the word, it is easy to see that all He said and did had reference to this. Philosophers talk about thinking in categories— the mind living, as it were, in a particular room with its own special furniture, pictures, and viewpoints, these giving a consistent direction and color to all that is there thought or expressed. It was in the category of the Kingdom that Christ's thought moved. Though one time He said He came to save the lost, or at another time to give men life, or to do His Father's will, these were all included among the objects of His Society.

No one can ever know what Christianity is till he has grasped this leading thought in the mind of

Christ. Peter and Paul have many wonderful and necessary things to tell us about what Christ was and did; but we are looking now at what Christ's own thought was. Do not think this is a mere modern theory. These are His own life-plans taken from His own lips. Do not allow any isolated text, even though it seem to sum up for you the Christian life, to keep you from trying to understand Christ's Program as a whole. The perspective of Christ's teaching is not everything, but without it everything will be distorted and untrue. There is much good in a verse, but often much evil. To see some small soul pirouetting throughout life on a single text, and judging all the world because it cannot find a partner, is not a Christian sight. Christianity does not grudge such souls their comfort. What it grudges is that they make Christ's Kingdom uninhabitable to thoughtful minds. Be sure that whenever the religion of Christ appears small, or forbidding, or narrow, or inhuman, you are dealing not with the whole —which is a matchless moral symmetry— nor even with an arch or column—for every detail is perfect—but with some cold stone removed from its place and suggesting nothing of the glorious structure from which it came.

Tens of thousands of persons who are familiar with religious truths have not noticed yet that Christ ever founded a Society at all. The reason is partly that people have read texts instead of reading their Bible, partly that they have studied Theology instead of studying Christianity, and partly because of the noiselessness and invisibility of the Kingdom of God itself. Nothing truer was ever said of this Kingdom than that "It cometh without observation." Its first discovery, therefore, comes to the Christian with all the force of a revelation. The sense of belonging to such a Society transforms life. It is the difference between being a solitary knight tilting single-handed, and often defeated, at whatever enemy one chances to meet on one's little acre of life, and the feel of belonging to a mighty army marching throughout all time to a certain victory. This note of universality given to even the humblest work we do, this sense of comradeship, this link with history, this thought of a definite campaign, this promise of success, is the possession of every obscurest unit in the Kingdom of God.

The Program of the Society

Hundreds of years before Christ's Society was formed, its Program had been issued to the world. I cannot think of any scene in history more dramatic than when Jesus entered the church in Nazareth and read it to the people. Not that when He appropriated to Himself that venerable fragment from Isaiah He was uttering a manifesto or announcing His formal Program. Christ never did things formally. We think of the words, as He probably thought of them, not in their old-world historical significance, nor as a full expression of His future aims, but as a summary of great moral facts now and always to be realized in the world since he appeared.

Remember as you read the words to what grim reality they refer. Recall what Christ's problem really was, what His Society was founded for. This

Program deals with a real world. Think of it as you read—not of the surface-world, but of the world as it is, as it sins and weeps, and curses and suffers and sends up its long cry to God. Limit it if you like to the world around your door, but think of it— of the city and the hospital and the dungeon and the graveyard, of the sweating-shop and the pawn-shop and the drink-shop; think of the cold, the cruelty, the fever, the famine, the ugliness, the loneliness, the pain. And then try to keep down the lump in your throat as you take up His Program and read—

To Bind up the Broken-hearted:
To Proclaim Liberty to the Captives:
To Comfort All That Mourn:
To Give unto Them—Beauty for Ashes,
The Oil of Joy for Mourning,
The Garment of Praise for the Spirit of Heaviness.

What an exchange—Beauty for Ashes, Joy for Mourning, Liberty for Chains! No marvel "the eyes of all them that were in the synagogue were fastened on Him" as He read; or that they "wondered at the gracious words which proceeded out of His lips." Only one man in that congregation, only one man in the world to-day could hear these accents with dismay—the man, the culprit, who has said hard words of Christ.

We are all familiar with the protest "Of course"—as if there were no other alternative to a person of culture—"Of course I am not a Christian, but I always speak respectfully of Christianity." Respectfully of Christianity! No remark fills one's soul with such sadness. One can understand a man as he reads these words being stricken speechless; one can see the soul within him rise to a white heat as each fresh benediction falls upon his ear and drive him, a half-mad enthusiast, to bear them to the world. But in what school has he learned of Christ who offers the Savior of the world his respect?

Men repudiate Christ's religion because they think it a small and limited thing, a scheme with no large human interests to commend it to this great social age. I ask you to note that there is not one burning interest of the human race which is not represented here. What are the great words of Christianity according to this Program? Take as specimens these:

Liberty,
Comfort,
Beauty,
Joy.

These are among the greatest words of life. Give them their due extension, the significance which Christ undoubtedly saw in them and which

Christianity undoubtedly yields, and there is almost no great want or interest of mankind which they do not cover.

These are not only the greatest words of life but they are the best. This Program, to those who have misread Christianity, is a series of surprises. Observe the most prominent note in it. It is gladness. Its first word is "good-tidings," its last is "joy." The saddest words of life are also there—but there as the diseases which Christianity comes to cure. No life that is occupied with such an enterprise could be other than radiant. The contribution of Christianity to the joy of living, perhaps even more to the joy of thinking, is unspeakable. The joyful life is the life of the larger mission, the disinterested life, the life of the overflow from self, the "more abundant life" which comes from following Christ. And the joy of thinking is the larger thinking, the thinking of the man who holds in his hand some Program for Humanity. The Christian is the only man who has any Program at all— any Program either for the world or for himself. Goethe, Byron, Carlyle taught Humanity much, but they had no Program for it. Byron's thinking was suffering; Carlisle's despair. Christianity alone exults. The belief in the universe as moral, the interpretation of history as progress, the faith in good as eternal, in evil as self-consuming, in humanity as evolving—these Christian ideas have transformed the malady of thought into a bounding hope. It was no sentiment but a conviction matured amid calamity and submitted to the tests of life that inspired the great modern poet of optimism to proclaim:—

"Gladness be with thee, Helper of the world!
I think this is the authentic sign and seal
Of Godship, that it ever waxes glad,
And more glad, until gladness blossoms, bursts
Into a rage to suffer for mankind
And recommence at sorrow."

But that is not all. Man's greatest needs are often very homely. And it is almost as much in its fearless recognition of the commonplace woes of life, and its deliberate offerings to minor needs, that the claims of Christianity to be a religion for Humanity stand. Look, for instance, at the closing sentence of this Program. Who would have expected to find among the special objects of Christ's solicitude the Spirit of Heaviness? Supreme needs, many and varied, had been already dealt with on this Program; many applicants had been met; the list is about to close. Suddenly the writer remembers the nameless malady of the poor—that mysterious disease which the rich share but cannot alleviate, which is too subtle for doctors, too incurable for Parliaments, too unpicturesque for philanthropy, too common even for sympathy. Can Christ meet that?

If Christianity could even deal with the world's Depression, could cure mere dull spirits, it would be the Physician of Humanity. But it can. It has the secret, a hundred secrets, for the lifting of the world's gloom. It cannot immediately remove the physiological causes of dulness— though obedience to its principles can do an infinity to prevent them, and its inspirations can do even more to lift the mind above them. But where the causes are moral or mental or social the remedy is in every Christian's hand. Think of any one at this moment whom the Spirit of Heaviness haunts. You think of a certain old woman. But you know for a fact that you can cure her. You did so, perfectly, only a week ago. A mere visit, and a little present, or the visit without any present, set her up for seven long days, and seven long nights. The machinery of the Kingdom is very simple and very silent, and the most silent parts do most, and we all believe so little in the medicines of Christ that we do not know what ripples of healing are set in motion when we simply smile on one another. Christianity wants nothing so much in the world as sunny people, and the old are hungrier for love than for bread, and the Oil of Joy is very cheap, and if you can help the poor on with a Garment of Praise, it will be better for them than blankets.

Or perhaps you know someone else who is dull—not an old woman this time, but a very rich and important man. But you also know perfectly what makes him dull. It is either his riches or his importance. Christianity can cure either of these though you may not be the person to apply the cure—at a single hearing. Or here is a third case, one of your own servants. It is a case of monotony. Prescribe more variety, leisure, recreation—anything to relieve the wearing strain. A fourth case—your most honored guest: Condition—leisure, health, accomplishments, means; Disease—Spiritual Obesity; Treatment—talent to be put out to usury. And so on down the whole range of life's dejection and ennui.

Perhaps you tell me this is not Christianity at all; that everybody could do that. The curious thing is that everybody does not. Good-will to men came into the world with Christ, and wherever that is found, in Christian or heathen land, there Christ is, and there His Spirit works. And if you say that the chief end of Christianity is not the world's happiness, I agree; it was never meant to be; but the strange fact is that, without making it its chief end, it wholly and infallibly, and quite universally, leads to it. Hence the note of Joy, though not the highest on Christ's Program, is a loud and ringing note, and none who serve in His Society can be long without its music. Time was when a Christian used to apologize for being happy. But the day has always been when he ought to apologize for being miserable.

Christianity, you will observe, really works. And it succeeds not only because it is divine, but because it is so very human—because it is common-sense. Why should the Garment of Praise destroy the Spirit of Heaviness? Because an old woman cannot sing and cry at the same moment. The Society of Christ is a sane Society. Its methods are rational. The principle in the old woman's case is simply that one emotion destroys another. Christianity works, as a railway man would say, with points. It switches souls from valley lines to mountain lines, not stemming the currents of life but diverting them. In the rich man's case the principle of cure is different, but it is again principle, not necromancy. His spirit of heaviness is caused, like any other heaviness, by the earth's attraction. Take away the earth and you take away the attraction. But if Christianity can do anything it can take away the earth. By the wider extension of horizon which it gives, by the new standard of values, by the mere setting of life's small pomps and interests and admirations in the light of the Eternal, it dissipates the world with a breath. All that tends to abolish worldliness tends to abolish unrest, and hence, in the rush of modern life, one far-reaching good of all even commonplace Christian preaching, all Christian literature, all which holds the world doggedly to the idea of a God and a future life, and reminds mankind of Infinity and Eternity.

Side by side with these influences, yet taking the world at a wholly different angle, works another great Christian force. How many opponents of religion are aware that one of the specific objects of Christ's society is Beauty? The charge of vulgarity against Christianity is an old one. If it means that Christianity deals with the ruder elements in human nature, it is true, and that is its glory. But if it means that it has no respect for the finer qualities, the charge is baseless. For Christianity not only encourages whatsoever things are lovely, but wars against that whole theory of life which would exclude them. It prescribes aestheticism. It proscribes asceticism. And for those who preach to Christians that in these enlightened days they must raise the masses by giving them noble sculptures and beautiful paintings and music and public parks, the answer is that these things are all already being given, and given daily, and with an increasing sense of their importance, by the Society of Christ. Take away from the world the beautiful things which have not come from Christ and you will make it poorer scarcely at all. Take away from modern cities the paintings, the monuments, the music for the people, the museums and the parks which are not the gifts of Christian men and Christian municipalities, and in ninety cases out of a hundred you will leave them unbereft of so much as a well-shaped lamp-post

It is impossible to doubt that the Decorator of the World shall not continue to serve to His later children, and in ever finer forms, the inspirations of beautiful things. More fearlessly than he has ever done, the Christian of modern life will use the noble spiritual leverages of Art. That this world, the people's world, is a bleak and ugly world, we do not forget; it is ever with us. But we esteem too little the mission of beautiful things in haunting the mind with higher thoughts and begetting the mood which leads to God. Physical beauty makes moral beauty. Loveliness does more than destroy ugliness; it destroys matter. A mere touch of it in a room, in a street, even on a door knocker, is a spiritual force. Ask the working-man's wife, and she will tell you there is a moral effect even in a clean table-cloth. If a barrel-organ in a slum can but drown a curse, let no Christian silence it. The mere light and color of the wall-advertisements are a gift of God to the poor man's somber world.

One Christmas-time a poor drunkard told me that he had gone out the night before to take his usual chance of the temptations of the street. Close to his door, at a shop window, an angel—so he said—arrested him. It was a large Christmas-card, a glorious white thing with tinsel wings, and as it glittered in the gas-light it flashed into his soul a sudden thought of Heaven. It recalled the earlier heaven of his infancy, and he thought of his mother in the distant glen, and how it would please her if she got this Christmas angel from her prodigal. With money already pledged to the devil he bought the angel, and with it a new soul and future for himself. That was a real angel. For that day as I saw its tinsel pinions shine in his squalid room I knew what Christ's angels were. They are all beautiful things, which daily in common homes are bearing up heavy souls to God.

But do not misunderstand me. This angel was made of pasteboard: a pasteboard angel can never save a soul. Tinsel reflects the sun, but warms nothing. Our Program must go deeper. Beauty may arrest the drunkard, but it cannot cure him.

It is here that Christianity asserts itself with a supreme individuality. It is here that it parts company with Civilization, with Politics, with all secular schemes of Social Reform. In its diagnosis of human nature it finds that which most other systems ignore; which, if they see, they cannot cure; which, left undestroyed, makes every reform futile, and every inspiration vain. That thing is Sin. Christianity, of all other philanthropies, recognizes that man's devouring need is Liberty—liberty to stop sinning; to leave the prison of his passions, and shake off the fetters of his past. To surround Captives with statues and pictures, to offer

Them-that-are-Bound a higher wage or a cleaner street or a few more cubic feet of air per head, is solemn trifling. It is a cleaner soul they want; a purer air, or any air at all, for their higher selves.

And where the cleaner soul is to come from apart from Christ I cannot tell. "By no political alchemy," Herbert Spencer tells us, "can you get golden conduct out of leaden instincts." The power to set the heart right, to renew the springs of action, comes from Christ. The sense of the infinite worth of the single soul, and the recoverableness of man at his worst, are the gifts of Christ. The freedom from guilt, the forgiveness of sins, come from Christ's Cross; the hope of immortality springs from Christ's grave. We believe in the gospel of better laws and an improved environment; we hold the religion of Christ to be a social religion; we magnify and call Christian the work of reformers, statesmen, philanthropists, educators, inventors, sanitary officers, and all who directly or remotely aid, abet, or further the higher progress of mankind; but in Him alone, in the fulness of that word, do we see the Savior of the world.

There are earnest and gifted lives to-day at work among the poor whose lips at least will not name the name of Christ. I speak of them with respect; their shoe-latchets many of us are not worthy to unloose. But because the creed of the neighboring mission-hall is a travesty of religion they refuse to acknowledge the power of the living Christ to stop man's sin, of the dying Christ to forgive it. O, narrowness of breadth! Because there are ignorant doctors do I yet rail at medicine or start an hospital of my own? Because the poor raw evangelist, or the narrow ecclesiastic, offer their little all to the poor, shall I repudiate all they do not know of Christ because of the little that they do know? Of gospels for the poor which have not some theory, state it how you will, of personal conversion one cannot have much hope. Personal conversion means for life a personal religion, a personal trust in God, a personal debt to Christ, a personal dedication to His cause. These, brought about how you will, are supreme things to aim at, supreme losses if they are missed. Sanctification will come to masses only as it comes to individual men; and to work with Christ's Program and ignore Christ is to utilize the sun's light without its energy.

But this is not the only point at which the uniqueness of this Society appears. There is yet another depth in humanity which no other system even attempts to sound. We live in a world not only of sin but of sorrow—

"There is no flock, however watched and tended,
But one dead lamb is there;
There is no home, howe'er defended,
But has one vacant chair."

When the flock thins, and the chair empties, who is to be near to heal? At that moment the gospels of the world are on trial. In the presence of death how will they act? Act! They are blotted out of existence. Philosophy, Politics, Reforms, are no more. The Picture Galleries close. The sculptures hide. The Committees disperse. There is crape on the door; the world withdraws. Observe, it withdraws. It has no mission.

So awful in its loneliness was this hour that the Romans paid a professional class; to step in with its mummeries and try to fill it. But that is Christ's own hour. Next to Righteousness the greatest word of Christianity is Comfort. Christianity has almost a monopoly of Comfort Renan was never nearer the mark than when he spoke of the Bible as "the great Book of the Consolation of Humanity." Christ's Program is full of Comfort, studded with Comfort: "to bind up the Broken-Hearted, to Comfort all that mourn, to Give unto them that mourn in Zion." Even the "good tidings" to the "meek" are, in the Hebrew, a message to the "afflicted" or "the poor." The word Gospel itself comes down through the Greek from this very passage, so that whatever else Christ's Gospel means it is first an Evangel for suffering men.

One note in this Program jars with all the rest. When Christ read from Isaiah that day He never finished the passage. A terrible word, Vengeance, yawned like a precipice across His path; and in the middle of a sentence "He closed the Book, and gave it again to the minister, and sat down". A Day of Vengeance from our God—these were the words before which Christ paused. When the prophet proclaimed it some great historical fulfilment was in his mind. Had the people to whom Christ read been able to understand its ethical equivalents He would probably have read on. For, so understood, instead of filling the mind with fear, the thought of this dread Day inspires it with a solemn gratitude. The work of the Avenger is a necessity. It is part of God's philanthropy.

For I have but touched the surface in speaking of the sorrow of the world as if it came from people dying. It comes from people living. Before ever the Broken-Hearted can be healed a hundred greater causes of suffering than death must be destroyed. Before the Captive can be free a vaster prison than his own sins must be demolished. There are hells on earth into which no breath of heaven can ever come; these must be swept away. There are social soils in which only unrighteousness can flourish; these must be broken up.

And that is the work of the Day of Vengeance. When is that day? It is now. Who is the Avenger? Law. What Law? Criminal Law, Sanitary Law, Social Law, Natural Law. Wherever the poor are trodden upon or tread upon one another; wherever the air is poison and the water foul; wherever want stares, and vice reigns, and rags rot—there the Avenger takes his stand. Whatever makes it more difficult for the drunkard to reform, for the children to be pure, for the widow to earn a wage, for any of the wheels of progress to revolve—with these he deals. Delay him not. He is the messenger of Christ. Despair of him not, distrust him not. His Day dawns slowly, but his work is sure. Though evil stalks the world, it is on the way to execution; though wrong reigns, it must end in self-combustion. The very nature of things is God's Avenger; the very story of civilization is the history of Christ's Throne.

Anything that prepares the way for a better social state is the fit work of the followers of Christ. Those who work on the more spiritual levels leave too much unhonored the slow toil of multitudes of unchurched souls who prepare the material or moral environments without which these higher labors are in vain. Prevention is Christian as well as cure; and Christianity travels sometimes by the most circuitous paths. It is given to some to work for immediate results, and from year to year they are privileged to reckon up a balance of success. But these are not always the greatest in the Kingdom of God. The men who get no stimulus from any visible reward, whose lives pass while the objects for which they toil are still too far away to comfort them; the men who hold aloof from dazzling schemes and earn the misunderstanding of the crowd because they foresee remoter issues, who even oppose a seeming good because a deeper evil lurks beyond—these are the statesmen of the Kingdom of God.

The Machinery of the Society

Such in dimmest outline is the Program of Christ's Society. Did you know that all this was going on in the world? Did you know that Christianity was such a living and purpose-like thing? Look back to the day when that Program was given, and you will see that it was not merely written on paper. Watch the drama of the moral order rise up, scene after scene, in history. Study the social evolution of humanity, the spread of righteousness, the amelioration of life, the freeing of slaves, the elevation of woman, the purification of religion, and ask what these can be if not the coming of the Kingdom of God on earth. For it is precisely through the movements of nations and the lives of men that this Kingdom comes. Christ might have done all this work Himself, with His own hands. But He did not. The crowning wonder of His scheme is that He entrusted it to men. It is the supreme glory of humanity that the machinery for its redemption should have been placed within itself. I think the saddest thing in Christ's life was that after founding a Society with aims so glorious He had to go away and leave it.

But in reality He did not leave it. The old theory that God made the world, made it as an inventor would make a machine, and then stood looking on to see it work, has passed away. God is no longer a remote spectator of the natural world, but immanent in it, pervading matter by His present Spirit, and ordering it by His Will. So Christ is immanent in men. His work is to move the hearts and inspire the lives of men, and through such hearts to move and reach the world. Men, only men, can carry out this work. This humanness, this inwardness, of the Kingdom is one reason why some scarcely see that it exists at all. We measure great movements by the loudness of their advertisement, or the place their externals fill in the public eye. This Kingdom has no externals. The usual methods of propagating a great cause were entirely discarded by Christ. The sword He declined; money He had none; literature He never used; the Church disowned Him; the State crucified Him. Planting His ideals in the hearts of a few poor men, He started them out unheralded to revolutionize the world. They did it by making friends and by making enemies; they went about, did good, sowed seed, died, and lived again in the lives of those they helped. These in turn, a fraction of them, did the same. They met, they prayed, they talked of Christ, they loved, they went among other men, and by act and word passed on their secret. The machinery of the Kingdom of God is purely social. It acts, not by commandment, but by contagion; not by fiat, but by friendship. "The Kingdom of God is like unto leaven, which a woman took and hid in three measures of meal till the whole was leavened."

After all, like all great discoveries once they are made, this seems absolutely the most feasible method that could have been devised. Men must live among men. Men must influence men. Organizations, institutions, churches, have too much rigidity for a thing that is to flood the world. The only fluid in the world is man. War might have won for Christ's cause a passing victory; wealth might have purchased a superficial triumph; political power might have gained a temporary success. But in these, there is no note of universality, of solidarity, of immortality. To live through the centuries and pervade the uttermost ends of the earth, to stand while kingdoms tottered and civilizations changed, to survive fallen churches and crumbling creeds—there was no soil for the Kingdom of God like the hearts of common men. Some who have written about this Kingdom have emphasized its moral grandeur, others its universality, others its adaptation to man's needs. One great writer speaks of its prodigious originality, another chiefly notices its success. I confess what almost strikes me most is the miracle of its simplicity.

Men, then, are the only means God's Spirit has of accomplishing His purpose. What men? You. Is it worth doing, or is it not? Is it worth while joining Christ's Society or is it not? What do you do all day? What is your personal stake in the coming of the Kingdom of Christ on earth? You are not interested in religion, you tell me; you do not care for your "soul". It was not about your religion I ventured to ask, still less about your soul. That you have no religion, that you do not care for your soul, does not absolve you from caring for the world in which you live. But you do not believe in this church, you reply, or accept this doctrine, or that. Christ does not, in the first instance, ask your thoughts, but your work. No man has a right to postpone his life for the sake of his thoughts. Why? Because this is a real world, not a think world. Treat it as a real world— act. Think by all means, but think also of what is actual, of what like the stern world is, of low much even you, creedless and churchless, could do to make it better. The thing to be anxious about is not to be right with man, but with mankind. And, so far as I know, there is nothing so on all fours with mankind as Christianity.

There are versions of Christianity, it is true, which no self-respecting mind can do other than disown—versions so hard, so narrow, so unreal, so super-theological, that practical men can find in them neither outlet for their lives nor resting-place for their thoughts. With these we have nothing to do. With these Christ had nothing to do— except to oppose them with every word and act of His life. It too seldom occurs to those who repudiate Christianity because of its narrowness or its unpracticalness, its sanctimoniousness or its dulness, that these were the very things which Christ strove against and unweariedly condemned. It was the one risk of His religion being given to the common people—an inevitable risk which He took without reserve—that its infinite luster should be tarnished in the fingering of the crowd or have its great truths narrowed into mean and unworthy molds as they passed from lip to lip. But though the crowd is the object of Christianity, it is not its custodian. Deal with the Founder of this great Commonwealth Himself. Any man of honest purpose who will take the trouble to inquire at first hand what Christianity really is, will find it a thing he cannot get away from. Without either argument or pressure, by the mere practicalness of its aims and the pathos of its compassions, it forces its August claim upon every serious life.

He who joins this Society finds himself in a large place. The Kingdom of God is a Society of the best men, working for the best ends, according to the best methods. Its membership is a multitude whom no man can number; its methods are as various as human nature; its field is the world. It is a Commonwealth, yet it honors a King; it is a Social Brotherhood, but it acknowledges the Fatherhood of God. Though not a Philosophy the world turns to it for light; though not Political it is the incubator of all great laws. It is more human than the State, for it deals with deeper needs; more Catholic than the Church, for it includes whom the Church rejects. It is a Propaganda, yet it works not by agitation but by ideals. It is a Religion, yet it holds the worship of God to be mainly the service of man. Though not a Scientific Society its watchword is Evolution; though not an Ethic it possesses the Sermon on the Mount. This mysterious Society owns no wealth but distributes fortunes. It has no minutes for history keeps them; no member's roll for no one could make it. Its entry-money is nothing; its subscription, all you have The Society never meets and it never adjourns. Its law is one word— loyalty; its Gospel one message — love. Verily "Whosoever will lose his life for My sake shall find it."

The Program for the other life is not out yet. For this world, for these faculties, for his one short life, I know nothing that is offered to man to compare with membership in the Kingdom of God. Among the mysteries which compass the world beyond, none is greater than how there can be in store for man a work more wonderful, a life more God-like than this. If you know anything better, live for it; if not, in the name of God and of Humanity, carry out Christ's plan.

www.ingramcontent.com/pod-product-compliance
Lightning Source LLC
Chambersburg PA
CBHW031659040426
42453CB00006B/344